CW01023846

AMAZINGLY POWERFUL MANTRAS

For 29 Specific Benefits

SHARADA SUBHASHINI

STARDOM BOOKS

STARDOM BOOKS

WORLDWIDE

www.StardomBooks.com

STARDOM BOOKS

A Division of Stardom Publishing

and infoYOGIS Technologies.

105-501 Silverside Road

Wilmington, DE 19809

FIRST EDITION FEBRUARY 2020

Stardom Books

AMAZINGLY POWERFUL MANTRAS

Sharada Subhashini

p. 106
cm. 12.7 x 20.3

Category: Spiritual/Self-help

PRICE:
INR 347
USD 4.95

ISBN-13: 978-1-7332116-5-9

SRI KRISHNA CHARANAM MAMAH:

DEDICATION

This book is dedicated to Lord Krishna - the love of my life; Lord Ganesha - my friend, philosopher and guide; my parents - A.N Ramachandar and Lalitha Ramachandar; and my daughter Medha

CONTENTS

SPECIFIC BENEFITS-WISE INDEX

1. To Remove Obstacles   5

2. To Get Quick Results   6

3. To Remove Unhappiness   6

4. To Pass Exams/Tests/Interviews   11

5. To Use As A Protective Shield   12

6. To Be Free Of Hunger   12

7. To Help Remain Gainfully Employed And To Progress In One's Career   13

8. To Remove All Fears   17

9. To Overcome Financial Problems   18

10. To Ensure All Around Success   23

11. To Invite Fortune And Good Luck   24

12. To Fight And Overcome All Illness   25

13. To Fight Enemies, Uncontrollable Events, Protection From Ghosts, Unidentified Weapons Or Illnesses   26

14. To Develop Intelligence And Blissfulness   29

15. To Resolve Issues By Having Time On Your Side   30

16. To Ward Off Untimely Death And For Healing,
    Rejuvenation and Nurturance   36

17. To Develop Inner And Physical Strength   37

18. To Get Our Wishes Fulfilled In 6 Months   52

19. For Protection Of All Kinds   57

20. To Overcome Ill Effects Of Rahu Maha Dasha
    In The Horoscope   62

21. To Get Spiritually Uplifted And Improvement
    In All Walks Of Life   63

22. To Overcome Self-Destructive Behavior   65

23. Mantra For Meditation   79

24. Prayers To Kanchi Periya Mahaswami   81

25. To Live A Long And Bountiful Life   83

26. To Rid Yourself Of Negative Karma   86

27. Morning Mantra – To Have A Great Day   87

28. To Sleep Well Without Any Nightmares   89

29. To Seek God For His Forgiveness   90

DEITY-WISE INDEX

1. Prayers To Lord Ganesh 05

2. Prayers To Devi Parvati 11

3. Prayers To Lord Narasimha 17

4. Prayers To Lord Vishnu 23

5. Prayers To Lord Shiva 29

6. Prayers To Lord Hanuman 37

7. Prayers To Lord Muruga/Subramanya 57

8. Prayers To The Sun God/Surya 63

9. Other Mantras 79

.

ACKNOWLEDGMENTS

I am grateful to the support of Lord Krishna in the making of this book. All the mantras in this book have been chosen by Him.

I am thankful for the unconditional love and support of my parents, daughter, siblings, sister-in-law, brothers-in-law, and my nieces and nephews. You are my worst critic, best buddies, my strength and my weakness. I love you all immensely.

PREFACE

There are millions of Mantras and several books on Mantras. However, people are unsure of which Mantra to recite for solving specific problems. This book bridges that gap and provides you with a ready reckoner of targeted Mantras for specific benefits.

You have not found this book – the book has found you. It will guide you out of your troubles and help you connect with the Supreme Power so that you may bask in His Glory and benefit from His Grace and blessings.

INTRODUCTION

ॐ श्री गणेशाय नमः
Om Shri Ganeshaya Namaha

गुरुः ब्रह्मा गुरुः विष्णु गुरुः देवो महेश्वरः |
गुरुः साक्षात्परब्रह्मा तस्मै श्री गुरुवे नमः ||

Guruh Brahma Guruh Vishnu
Guruh Devo Maheshwaraaya
Guruh Saakshaath Parabrahma
Thasmai Shree Gurave Namaha

Life is not easy. Every person goes through several challenges in the course of their life. Some of these challenges are within our control, and some of them are caused by circumstances beyond our control. To tackle issues that we think are beyond our control, have no solution, or that we need divine guidance/interference, mantras are the best tool.

Mantras work. Whether you believe in them or not. Whether you know its meaning or not.

Like any sound or thought wave, a mantra is a vibration. Like any vibration, it creates a ripple effect when formed. Like any vibration, it affects your mind and body even if you do not believe in its existence or hear/see/feel it. A good example of this is a radio frequency, which is a vibration that you cannot see but can hear or a TV signal which you can see but not feel. Nevertheless, these vibrations do affect the mind and body.

Prayers and Faith – Both are invisible. But both have so much energy to convert the impossible to the possible!

When we stand in a pool of water and a stone is thrown into it, the ripple that is formed will affect you depending on the strength of the ripple. If it is a mild ripple, the effect will not be significant. But if it is a really strong ripple caused by a large stone, the effect could even topple you and make you fall into the water!

The strength of the ripple itself is determined by the strength or power of the stone that is cast into the water. The stronger the stone, the greater the ripple. The ripple that is caused is a fact and a reality whether we choose to acknowledge or believe in it or not.

It is common knowledge that more than 75% of our body and mind constitute liquids/water. Mantras are stones that we cast into the waters of our body and mind. Depending on the strength of the mantras, ripples are formed within us and these vibrations work on our mind and body to produce the desired effect. Some mantras cause small ripples and take time to cause an effect while others cause large ripples and we can feel its effect and benefit almost immediately.

There are millions of mantras and several books on mantras. However, people are unsure of which mantra to recite for solving specific problems. This book bridges that gap and provides you with a handbook/ready reckoner of targeted mantras for specific benefits.

Here is a compilation of some very powerful mantras that can affect us very strongly and give us some amazing benefits. When repeatedly recited or read, these mantras can produce the desired results very quickly. They are simple to recite and do not need a degree in Sanskrit!

You have not found this book – the book has found you. Similarly, I do not claim to have written this book. All these mantras have allowed me to collect them and put them together in this book. There is a reason for this. The purpose of your finding this book is to guide you out of your troubles and to help you connect with the Supreme Power so that you may bask in His Glory and benefit from His Grace and blessings.

You do not have to recite all of the mantras in this book every day. Just pick a mantra that is specific to your needs and watch yourself reap its benefits! It works! Try it and see! But first, I would recommend that you read the entire book to decide the best mantra to help you with the problem that you are immediately facing.

A good way of increasing the speed of your results would be to repeat the mantra in the same place and at the same time every day. This creates a concentration of vibrations until the momentum is gathered sufficient enough to operate hidden laws and bring about the desired result. It will ensure that you get your results faster. But for those of you for whom this is not possible, don't lose heart! Just repeat your chosen mantra everyday whenever you can until your wishes manifest.

I pray to the almighty that God blesses everyone with health, wealth, and happiness.

सर्वजनोसुखिनोभवन्तु
Sarve Jano Sukhino Bhavanthu

**With lots of love and best wishes,
Sharada Subhashini**

1. PRAYERS TO LORD GANESH

1. To remove obstacles

This is a popular Ganesh mantra to invoke the benevolent Lord's blessings. It is one of the mantras frequently recited by Hindus. It describes Lord Ganesh as one with a curved trunk and a mighty body, who has the magnificence of a million suns. Lord Ganesh is also the most widely worshipped deity amongst the Hindus, and He is believed to be the remover of obstacles from our lives.

वक्रतुण्ड महाकाय सूर्यकोटि समप्रभ ।
निर्विघ्नं कुरु मे देव सर्वकार्येषु सर्वदा ॥

Vakratunda mahakaaya
Suryakoti samaprabha
Nirvighnam kuru mey deva
Sarva kaaryeshu sarvada

2. To get quick results

This mantra literally says," Oh Ganesha, please give me the quick results that I seek."

ॐ गं गणपतये नमः
ॐ क्षिप्र प्रसादाय नमः

Om gam ganapatayenamaha
Om kshipra prasaadaaya namaha

3. To remove all unhappiness

Sankata Naashaka Ganesha Stotra - This literally means "The Ganesha Mantra that removes unhappiness." This mantra is from the Narada Purana. It is an Ashatakam – which means it has 8 paragraphs. The 7th paragraph mentions that without any doubt (definitely), it provides results within one month.

प्रणम्य शिरसा देवं गौरीपुत्र विनायकम् ।
भक्ता वासं स्मरेन्नित्यायु ष्कामार्थसिद्धये ॥१॥

Pranamya shirasa devam
Gauri putra vinayakam
Bhakthya vyasa smaren nithyam
Aayuh kaama artha sidhaye

प्रथमं वक्रतुण्डं च एकदन्तं द्वितीयकम् ।
तृतीयं कृष्णपिङ्गाक्षं गजवक्त्रं चतुर्थकम् ॥२॥

Prathamam vakra thundam cha
Ekadantham dveethiyakam
Trithiyam Krishna pingaaksham
Gajavakthram chathurthakam

लम्बोदरं पञ्चमं च षष्ठं विकटमेव च ।
सप्तमं विघ्नराजं च धूम्रवर्ण तथाष्टमम् ॥३॥

Lambhodaram panchamam cha
Sashtam vikatam eva cha
Sapthamam vignaraajam cha
Dhoomra varna thathaashta mam

नवमं भालचन्द्रं च दशमं तु विनायकम् ।
एकादशं गणपतिं द्वादशं तु गजाननम् ॥४॥

Navamam baala chandram cha
Dasamam thu vinayakam
Ekaadasam ganapathim
Dwaadasaam thu gajananam

द्वादशैतानि नामानि त्रिसन्ध्यं यः पठेन्नरः ।
न च विघ्नभयं तस्य सर्वसिद्धिश्च जायते ॥५॥

Dwaadasaithaani naamani
Trisandhyam yah paten narah
Na cha vighna bhayam thasya
Sarva siddhischa jaayate

विद्यार्थी लभते विद्यां धनार्थी लभते धनम् ।
पुत्रार्थी लभते पुत्रान्मोक्षार्थी लभते गतिम् ॥६॥

Vidyaarthi labhathe vidhyaam
Dhanarthi labhathe dhanam
Puthrarthi labhathe puthram
Moksharthi labhathe gatheem

जपेद् गणपतिस्तोत्रं षड्भिर्मासैः फलं लभेत् ।
संवत्सरेण सिद्धिं च लभते नात्र संशयः ॥७॥

Japeth ganapathi sthothram
Shadbhir masai phalam labeth
Samvatsarena sidhim cha
Labhathe na athra samsayah

अष्टाभ्यो ब्राह्मणेभ्यश्च लिखित्वा यः समर्पयेत् ।
तस्य विद्या भवेत्सर्वा गणेशस्य प्रसादतः ॥८॥

Ashtaabhyo braahmanebyas cha
Likithwa yah samarpayeth
Thasya vidhya bhaveth sarvaa
Ganeshasya prasaadath

AMAZINGLY POWERFUL MANTRAS

2. PRAYERS TO DEVI PARVATI

1. To Pass in your exams/tests/interviews

Along with preparing for your exams/tests/interviews, chanting this mantra 108 times will ensure that you get the benefits of your hard work, and you will pass in flying colours. At the age of 55, when I took up an international exam, I was doubtful if I could pass the exam as memorising the material was a huge challenge. And then – this mantra found me! Along with my studying, I also started repeating this 108 times daily. And guess what – I passed with a merit score!!!

अम्बिका अनादि निधना अश्वारूढ़ अपराजिता

Ambika anaadhi nidanaa ashwaroodaa aparaajithaa

2. To use as a protective shield

This mantra is the Vedic equivalent of the Reiki shield. Please create a mental vision about the object (s) that you would like to place into the protective shield. It could be you, your spouse, children, house, vehicle – it could be anything at all. Just recite this mantra while visualizing it as surrounding the object (s) in the protective shield. This protection lasts for 24 hours. It will protect against everything – robbery, accidents, theft, loss, etc.

ॐ श्री दुर्गे दुर्गे रक्षिणी म्स्वाहा ।

Om Sri Durge Durge Rakshineem Swaha

3. To ensure you do not go hungry or suffer from want of Groceries or Food

Food is one of the basic necessities of life. There is a saying in Hindu Philosophy – "Annam Para

Brahmam" – i.e., Food is God. Annapurna is an incarnation of Goddess Parvati, who is the wife of Lord Shiva. She is the Hindu Goddess of food and cooking. Annapurna is empowered with the ability to supply unlimited food to all.

अन्नपूर्णे सदापूर्णे शङ्करप्राणवल्लभे।
ज्ञानवैराग्यसिद्ध्यर्थं भिक्षां देहि च पार्वति॥

Annapurne sadaa purne
Shankara praana vallabhe
Gnaana vairaagya siddhyartham
Bhikshaam dehi cha Paarvate

4. To help remain gainfully employed and to progress in one's career

Nemili Bala

Nemili is a small town in Tamil Nadu. The temple of Bala Tripurasundari is well known among the people of the area as an immensely beautiful and tiny goddess in the form of a nine-year-old girl. She is the "go to" goddess to solve problems related to our employment. People who have lost their jobs due to redundancy or redeployment programs flock to see her. This mantra of Bala Tripurasundari will ensure that you will be able to get the job that you are passionate about and also help you to retain it. In the unfortunate event that you do face employment related issues, this mantra will help you to find a solution. A word of caution please do not bargain with the goddess that "If I get a job, I will do puja in your temple, etc.". Just mention what you would like her to help you with and leave the rest to her. Once the wish has been granted, visit her temple and thank her. As Bala Tripurasundari is Parvati in the form of a child, you are allowed to carry some chocolates, fruits, and flowers and worship her with the love that you would show to a baby girl. The temple priests also distribute chocolates as Prasad! When I lost my job, I could not get another one despite several attempts and powerful references. It was then that I heard about this temple and this wonderful goddess. Within one month of visiting her the first time, I got the job of my choice. The awe and respect that I have for her has now turned into a deep love, and I am unable to refrain from seeing her every once in few months. Of course, the fact that I live fairly nearby in Bangalore helps me to visit her often. In case you are unable to visit her, please visualise her picture and pray to her. She hears all and sees all and is very receptive to our prayers.

बाला त्रिपुरसुंदरी मूल मंत्र

Bala Tripurasundari Moola Mantra

जं क्लीम सोव
सोव क्लीम जं
जं क्लीम सोव

Jum Kleem Sov
Sov Kleem Jum
Jum Kleem Sov

3. PRAYERS TO LORD NARASIMHA

1. To remove all fears

It is said that this mantra is the essence of all kavach mantras or mantras meant for wearing in a kavach (capsule). The mantra is written on a small piece of bark and then sealed in the capsule with a Tulasi (Holy Basil) leaf or petals from flowers that have been offered to the idol of Lord Narasimha. After worshipping the Lord Narasimha, the Lord is requested to reside in the kavach. Then it has full protective power. Men can wear the kavach around the neck or on the upper right arm, while women wear it around the neck or on the upper left arm. The kavach may be worn in all circumstances, at any time, or in any place.

This kavach is worn to rid you of all fears of any kind. If unable to wear such a kavach, the same effect is achieved by reciting the mantra. During times of fear or a lack of courage to face a situation, please recite this mantra, and you will find yourself stronger and more confident to face the situation on hand.

उग्रं वीरं महा विष्णुं ज्वलन्तं सर्वतोमुखं ।
नृसिंहम भीषणं भद्रं मृत्योऱ मृत्युं नमाम्यहम् ।।

Ugram viram maha vishnum
Jvalantam sarvato mukham
Nrisimham bheeshanam bhadram
Mrutyor mrutyum namamyaham

2. To overcome financial problems

This is a powerful shloka that, when recited regularly, will relieve people of their debts and insolvency however severe and acute. In ancient Indian texts, it is said that reciting this mantra will remove poverty and financial troubles within 6 months of continuous recitation. This mantra is also an Ashtakam – meaning it has 8 stanzas or paragraphs. The last paragraph mentions that reciting this mantra will give you money very quickly.

ॐ महालक्ष्म्यै च विद्महेविष्णुपत्यै च धीमहि
तन्नो लक्ष्मी प्रचोदयात् ॥

Om Mahalakshmai cha vidymahe
Vishnu patni cha dhimahi
Tanno Lakshmi prachodayaath

ॐ देवता कार्यसिध्यर्थं सभास्तम्भसमुद्भवम्।
श्रीनृसिंहं महावीरं नमामि ऋणमुक्तये॥१॥

Om Devata karya sidhyartham
Sabhasthambha samudbhavam
Sri Nrisimham mahaveeram
Namami runa mukthaye

लक्ष्म्यालिङ्गितवामाङ्गं भक्तानाम् वरदायकम्।
श्रीनृसिंहं महावीरं नमामि ऋणमुक्तये॥२॥

Lakshmya aalingitha vamangam
Bhakthanaam vara dayakam
Sri Nrisimham mahaveeram
Namami runa mukthaye

अन्त्रमालाधरं शङ्खचक्राब्जायुधधारिणम्।
श्रीनृसिंहं महावीरं नमामि ऋणमुक्तये॥३॥

Aantramaladaram sankha
Chakrabja aayudarinim
Sri Nrisimham mahaveeram
Namami runa mukthaye

स्मरणात्सर्वपापघ्नं कद्रुजं विषनाशनम्।
श्रीनृसिंहं महावीरं नमामि ऋणमुक्तये॥५॥

Smaranath sarva papagnam
Khadruja visha nasanam
Sri Nrisimham mahaveeram
Namami runa mukthaye

सिंहनादेन महत्ता दिग्दन्ति भयनाशनम्।
श्रीनृसिंहं महावीरं नमामि ऋणमुक्तये॥४॥

Simhanaade namahatha
Digdanthi bhayanasanam
Sri Nrisimham mahaveeram
Namami runa mukthaye

प्रह्लादवरदं श्रीशं दैतेश्वरविदारणम्।
श्रीनृसिंहं महावीरं नमामि ऋणमुक्तये॥६॥

Prahlada varadam srisam
Daithyeswara vidharanam
Sri Nrisimham mahaveeram
Namami runa mukthaye

क्रूरग्रहैही पीडितानाम्भक्तानाम् अभय प्रदम्
श्रीनृसिंहं महावीरं नमामि ऋण मुक्तये ॥ ७॥

Krooragrahaih peedithaanam
Bhakthanam abhayapradham
Sri Nrisimham mahaveeram
Namami runa mukthaye

वेद वेदांत यज्ञेशं ब्रह्मरुद्रादिवंदितम्।
श्रीनृसिंहं महावीरं नमामि ऋणमुक्तये॥८॥

Veda vedantha yajnesam
Brahma rudradhi vandhitham
Sri Nrisimham mahaveeram
Namami runa mukthaye.

इदं यो पठते नित्यं ऋणमोचन संजितम्
अनृणीजायते सद्यो धनं शीघ्रमवाप्नुयात् ॥९॥

Idam yo pathathe nithyam
Runa mochana sanjitham
Anrni jayathe sathyor
Dhanam sheegram avapnuyath

4. PRAYERS TO LORD VISHNU

1. To ensure success in all that we do

This is a prayer that literally means "Lord Krishna – I surrender to you." When I visited the temple of Srinathji in Rajasthan, I had the good fortune of interacting with the Head Priest of this temple. His advice to me was that before I begin any activity, I should utter this mantra and dedicate the results to Krishna. I must mention that I have been doing it ever since with excellent results. Of course, there have been times when the result was not in my favour, but in hindsight, I have realised that it was in my interest when the result has not been in my favour. Many a time things have moved along so smoothly that I can only put it down to divine intervention!

श्री कृष्ण शरणम ममः
श्री कृष्ण शरणम ममः
श्री कृष्ण शरणम ममः

Shri Krishna sharanam mamaha
Shri Krishna sharanam mamaha
Shri Krishna sharanam mamaha

2. To invite fortune and good luck

This mantra is a summarized version of the Vishnu Sahasranaama. It is said that if we recite this mantra 3 times, we get the full benefit of reciting the entire Vishnu Sahasranaama.

Chanting the Vishnu Sahasranaama regularly can help invite fortune and good luck inside the household. It also helps overcome financial losses, relaxes the mind, and frees it from unwanted worries and distracting thoughts allowing it to focus on positive thoughts. It increases the health and happiness of the children. The names of Lord Vishnu are like a very powerful shield to guard you against all negative energies, bad luck, misfortune, dangers, black magic, accidents, and the evil eye. It safeguards the mind and body from the evil plans of enemies.

Vishnu Sahasranaama can help cure incurable diseases. It can help overcome negative states of mind, including fear, stress, tension, anxiety and low self-esteem.

The home where this mantra is chanted will find peace and prosperity.

श्री राम राम रामेति रमे रामे मनोरमे । सहस्रनाम तत्तुल्यं रामनाम वरानने ॥

Shri raama raama raameti
Rame raame manorame
Sahasranama tattulyam
Raama naama varaanane

3. To fight and overcome all illnesses, even incurable ones

This mantra has been taken from the Narayaneeyam. It is the last shloka in the 8th Chapter of this book, which is about Sri Krishna or Guruvayurappan – the Lord of Guruvayur. Kanchi Periya Mahaswami has mentioned in one of his lectures that reciting this prayer 108 times for 48 days will ensure that one is cured of any illness – even cancer. But it can be recited even once every day for overall health. It is recommended that you place a cup of water in front of you while reciting this mantra and then drink the water once the chanting is complete.

अस्मि न्परात्म त्रनु पाद्मकल्पे
त्वमित्थमुत्थापितपद्मयोनि: ।
अनन्तभूमा मम रोगराशिं
निरुन्धि वातालयवास विष्णो

Asmin paraathman nanu paadmakalpae
Thvamiththa muththaapitha padmayonihi
Anantha bhoomaa mama rogaraashim
Nirundhi vaathaalayavaasa vishno

4. **To rid oneself of the miseries caused by enemies, uncontrollable events, protection from ghosts, unidentified illnesses and weapons**

Maha Sudarshana mantra is a powerful shloka addressed to Lord Vishnu as Sudarshana. This mantra is recited to invoke the protection of Vishnu as the bearer of the Sudarshana Chakra. It is also the mantra, which is recited 1008 times while performing the Maha Sudarshana Homa or Havan.

ओं श्रीम् ह्रीं क्लीम्
श्रीकृष्णाय गोविंदाय
गोपीजन वल्लभाय
पराय परमपुरुषाय परमात्मने
परकर्म मंत्र यंत्र तंत्र
औषध अस्त्र शस्त्राणि संहारा संहारा
मृत्यो मोचय मोचय
आयु र्वर्धय वर्धय
शत्रू त्राशय नाशय
ओं नमो भगवते महासुदर्शनाय
दीपत्रे ज्वाला परिताय
सर्वधि क्ष्णोभण कराया
हूं फट्ब्रह्मणे परंज्योतिषे स्वाहा

Om shreem hreem kleem
Shree krishnaaya govindaaya
Gopi jana vallabhaaya
Paraya paramapurashaaya paramathmane
Para karma mantra tantra yantra
Oushada astra shastrani samhara samhara
Mruthyor mochaya mochaya
Aayur vardhaya vardhaya
Shatroon naashaya naashaya
Om namo bhagavathe mahasudarshanaaya
Deeptre jwaala parithaaya
Sarva dhikshobhana karaaaya
Hoom phat brahmane paranjyothishe swaaha

5. PRAYERS TO LORD SHIVA

1. To develop intelligence and blissfulness

Lord Shiva is one of the Godheads in the Hindu Trinity, along with Brahma and Vishnu. He is considered as the destroyer of evil. He is easily pleased with devotion and bhakti and gives boons and grants wishes to his devotees very quickly.

He is also the patron God of yoga, meditation, and arts and is also known as Adi yogi. As Nataraja – the Lord of Dance, Shiva performs the Ananda Tandava (dance of bliss), a dance in which the universe is created, maintained, and dissolved. He is also known as Pashupatinath, as he protects animals from disease and distress.

This mantra is a high frequency mantra and generates several sound waves per second. Reciting it ensures that the sound waves bring our intelligence to the highest level. Repeating the mantra slowly during meditation promotes harmony, concentration, and mental strength.

This Shiva panchakshara (pancha 5, akshara–syllables panchakshara means having 5 syllables–Om Naamh Shiva aa yah) mantra helps you to connect with Lord Shiva and Sages all over the world are constantly meditating upon or chanting this auspicious mantra and increasing their abilities to infinite levels.

ॐ नमः शिवाय
ॐ नमः शिवाय
ॐ नमः शिवाय

OM NAMAH SHIVAAYA
OM NAMAH SHIVAAYA
OM NAMAH SHIVAAYA

2. To resolve issues by having time on your side

The Kalabhairavaashtakam was written by Adi Shankaracharya. It also has 8 stanzas in praise of Shiva in His Kalabhairava form. The word Kaala means time, and Bhairava is another name for Lord Shiva. So Kaalabhairava is Shiva, who controls time. In this form, Shiva has a dog as his vehicle.

Chanting this mantra with faith, love, and devotion helps a person to resolve issues with time on your side. You will feel a sense of self control and will be filled with positive energy.

This verse in the last stanza mentions Shokha moha loba dhainya kopa taapa naashanam. It means reciting this mantra will destroy your anger, desires, greediness, miseries, and all your sins.

Kaalabhairava Ashtakam

देवराजसेव्यमानपावनांघ्रिपङ्कजं
व्यालयज्ञसूत्रमिन्दुशेखरं कृपाकरम् ।
नारदादियोगिवृन्दवन्दितं दिगंबरं
काशिकापुराधिनाथकालभैरवं भजे ॥१॥

Deva raja sevyamaana paavana
angghripangkajam
Vyaala yajnya sutram indu shekharam
Krpaakaram
Naaradaadi yogi vrnda vanditam
digambaram
Kaashikaapuraa dhinaatha Kaalabhairavam
bhaje

भानुकोटिभास्वरं भवाब्धितारकं परं
नीलकण्ठमीप्सितार्थदायकं त्रिलोचनम् ।
कालकालमंबुजाक्षमक्षशूलमक्षरं
काशिकापुराधिनाथकालभैरवं भजे ॥२॥

Bhaanu koti bhaasvaram bhavaabdhi
taarakam param
Neela kantta ipsithaartha daayakam
trilochanam
Kaala kaalam ambujaaksham aksha shoolam
aksharam
Kaashikaapuraa dhinaatha Kaalabhairavam
bhaje

शूलटङ्कपाशदण्डपाणिमादिकारणं
श्यामकायमादिदेवमक्षरं निरामयम् ।
भीमविक्रमं प्रभुं विचित्रताण्डवप्रियं
काशिकापुराधिनाथकालभैरवं भजे ॥३॥

Shoola tangka pasha danda paani maadi
kaaranam
Shyaama Kaayamaadi devam akshsaram
niraamayam
Bheema vikramam prabhum vichitra
taandava priyam
Kaashikaapuraa dhinaatha Kaalabhairavam
Bhaje

भुक्तिमुक्तिदायकं प्रशस्तचारुविग्रहं
भक्तवत्सलं स्थितं समस्तलोकविग्रहम् ।
विनिकणन्मनोज्ञहेमकिङ्किणीलसत्कटिं
काशिकापुराधिनाथकालभैरवं भजे ॥४॥

Bhukti mukti daayakam prashasta chaaru
vigraham
Bhakta vatsalam sthitam samasta loka
vigraham
Vi nikvanan manojnya hema kingkinnee lasat
kattim
Kaashikaapuraa dhinaatha Kaalabhairavam
bhaje

धर्मसेतुपालकं त्वधर्ममार्गनाशकं
कर्मपाशमोचकं सुशर्मदायकं विभुम् ।
स्वर्णवर्णशेषपाशशोभिताङ्गमण्डलं
काशिकापुराधिनाथकालभैरवं भजे ॥५॥

Dharma setu paalakam swadharma maarga
naashakam
Karma pasha mochakam susharma
daayakam vibhum
Swarna varna shesha pasha shobhitaanga
mandalam
Kaashikaapuraa dhinaatha Kaalabhairavam
bhaje

रत्नपादुकाप्रभाभिरामपादयुग्मकं
नित्यमद्वितीयमिष्टदैवतं निरंजनम् ।
मृत्युदर्पनाशनं करालदंष्ट्रमोक्षणं
काशिकापुराधिनाथकालभैरवं भजे ॥६॥

Ratnapaadukaa prabhaabhi raama paada
yugmakam
Nityam adviteeyam ishta daivatam
niranjanam
Mrtyu darpa naashanam karaala damshttra
mokshanam
Kaashikaapuraa dhinaatha Kaalabhairavam
bhaje

अट्टहासभिन्नपद्मजाण्डकोशसंततिं
दृष्टिपातनष्टपापजालमुग्रशासनम् ।
अष्टसिद्धिदायकं कपालमालिकाधरं
काशिकापुराधिनाथकालभैरवं भजे ॥७॥

Atta haasa bhinna padma jaanda kosha
santatim
Drushti paatha nashta papa jaalam ugra
shaasanam
Ashta siddhi daayakam kapaala maalikaa
dharam
Kaashikaapuraa dhinaatha Kaalabhairavam
bhaje

भूतसंघनायकं विशालकीर्तिदायकं
काशिवासलोकपुण्यपापशोधकं विभुम् ।
नीतिमार्गकोविदं पुरातनं जगत्पतिं
काशिकापुराधिनाथकालभैरवं भजे ॥८॥

Bhootha sanghnaayakam vishaala
Keerthi daayakam
Kaashi vaasa loka punya paapa shodhakam
vibhum
Neeti maarga kovidam puraatanam
jagatpatim
Kaashikaapuraa dhinaatha Kaalabhairavam
bhaje

कालभैरवाष्टकं पठंति ये मनोहरं
ज्ञानमुक्तिसाधनं विचित्रपुण्यवर्धनम् ।
शोकमोहदैन्यलोभकोपतापनाशनं
ए प्रयान्ति कालभैरवांघ्रिसन्निधिं ध्रुवम् ॥९॥

Kaalabhairava ashtakam patanti ye
manoharam
Gnyaana mukti saadhanam vichitra punya
vardhanam
Shoka moha dainya lobha kopa taapa
naashanam
Ye prayaanti kaalabhairavaanghri sannidhim
dhruvam

3. To ward off untimely death and for healing rejuvenation and nurturance

This mantra is a moksha mantra that bestows longevity and immortality and helps to conquer death. As this prayer is to Lord Thryambakam – or Lord Shiva with the third eye, when faced with death, it opens one's spiritual third eye and brings calmness and spiritual awakening. Regular chanting of this mantra guards us against untimely death, critical illnesses, and evil spirits

महामृत्युंजय मन्त्रः
Maha Mrityunjaya Mantraha

ॐ त्र्यम्बकं यजामहे
सुगन्धिं पुष्टिवर्धनम् ।
उर्वारुकमिव बन्धनान्
मृत्योर्मुक्षीय मामृतात् ॥

Om thryambakam yajaamahe
Sugandhim pushti vardhanam
Urvaarukamiva bandhanaath
Mrtyor muksheeya maamruthaat

6. PRAYERS TO LORD HANUMAN

1. To develop inner and physical strength

Hanuman is a deity with extraordinary powers and strength. To be free of the presence of evil spirits, ghosts, black magic, fear of any kind, nightmares, and when you need any kind of strength to face an unpleasant situation, recitation of Hanuman Chalisa provides excellent results and protection. The word Chalisa means 40 in Hindi. Hanuman Chalisa is 40 stanzas about Hanuman, including describing him, the powers he possesses and the benefits that come with reciting this.

According to legends, the lord of Saturn, Shani Dev, had given a boon to Hanuman that his devotees will be spared from negative karmic effects. Therefore, reciting Hanuman Chalisa helps reduce the effects of Sade Sati or the dreaded 7 and a half years of the astrological cycle. So those who are suffering due to the placement of Saturn in their horoscope should chant the Hanuman Chalisa, especially on Saturdays for peace and prosperity.

If you have nightmares, place a Hanuman Chalisa book under your pillow or bed to sleep peacefully. Lord Hanuman also prevents accidents and ensures the success of any trip. This is why we can find tiny figurines or pictures of Hanuman placed in most vehicles in India.

Like Lord Ganesha, Hanuman also has the reputation of removing all our obstacles. Reading the Hanuman Chalisa helps you feel relaxed and completely in control of your life and can fill a person with divine bliss. It also cures small lifestyle ailments such as headache, sleeplessness, anxiety, depression, etc.

Reciting Hanuman Chalisa also helps in reforming people who have fallen into bad company or have become slaves to an objectionable habit.

Prayer To The Great Guru or Master

श्रीगुरु चरन सरोज रज निज मनु मुकुरु सुधारि।
बरनउँ रघुबर बिमल जसु जो दायकु फल चारि॥

Shri Guru charan saroj raj, nij man mukut
sudhar
Varnau raghubar vimal yash, jo dayak phal
char

बुद्धिहीन तनु जानिके, सुमिरौं पवन कुमार
बल बुधि विद्या देहु मोहि, हरहु कलेश विकार

Buddhihin tanu janike, simrau pavankumar
Balbudhi vidya dehu mohi, harahu kalesh
vicar

Hanuman Chalisa

जय हनुमान ज्ञान गुन सागर
जय कपीस तिहुँ लोक उजागर॥१॥

Jai Hanuman gyan gun sagar
Jai kapisa tihun lok ujagar

रामदूत अतुलित बल धामा
अंजनि-पुत्र पवनसुत नामा॥२॥

Ramdut atulit bal dhama
Anjaniputra pavansut nama

महाबीर विक्रम बजरंगी
कुमति निवार सुमति के संगी॥३॥

Mahavir vikram bajrangi
Kumati nivar sumati ke sangi

कंचन वरन विराज सुबेसा
कानन कुंडल कुँचित केसा॥४॥

Kanchan varan viraj subesa
Kanan kundal kunchit keshae

हाथ वज्र और ध्वजा बिराजे
काँधे मूँज जनेऊ साजे॥५॥

Hath vajra aur dhvaja birajai
kandhe munj janeu saaje

शंकर सुवन केसरी नंदन
तेज प्रताप महा जगवंदन॥६॥

Shankar suvan kesarinandan
Tej pratap mahajag vandan

विद्यावान गुनी अति चातुर
रामकाज करिबे को आतुर॥७॥

Vidyavan guni ati chatur
Ram kajkaribe ko atur

प्रभु चरित्र सुनिबे को रसिया
राम लखन सीता मनबसिया॥८॥

Prabhu charitra sunibe ko rasiya
Ram lakhan sita man basiya

सूक्ष्म रूप धरि सियहि दिखावा
विकट रूप धरि लंक जरावा॥९॥

Sukshma rup dhari siyaahi dikhava
Vikat rup dhari Lanka jaravaa

भीम रूप धरि असुर संहारे
रामचंद्र के काज संवारे॥१०॥

Bhim rup dhari asur samhare
Ramchandra ke kaj savare

लाय संजीवन लखन जियाए
श्री रघुबीर हरषि उर लाए॥११॥

Laaya sanjivan lakhan jiyaye
Shri raghubir harashi ur laaye

रघुपति कीन्ही बहुत बड़ाई
तुम मम प्रिय भरत हि सम भाई॥१२॥

Raghupati kinhi bahut badhai
Tum mama priya bharat hi sam bhai

सहस बदन तुम्हरो यश गावै
अस कहि श्रीपति कंठ लगावै॥१३॥

Sahas badan tumharo yash gavai
Asa kahi shripati kanth lagavain

सनकादिक ब्रह्मादि मुनीशा
नारद शारद सहितअहीशा॥१४॥

Sanakaadika brahmaadi munisha
Naarad saarad sahita ahishaa

यम कुबेर दिगपाल जहाँ ते
कवि कोविद कहि सके कहाँ ते॥१५॥

Yam kuber digpal jahante
Kavi kovid kahi sakai kahaante

तुम उपकार सुग्रीवहि कीन्हा
राम मिलाय राजपद दीन्हा॥१६॥

Tum upkar sugrivahin kinha
Ram milaaya rajpad dinha

तुम्हरो मंत्र बिभीषण माना
लंकेश्वर भये सब जग जाना॥१७॥

Tumharo mantra vibhishan mana
Lankeshvar bhaye sabh jag jana

जुग सहस्त्र जोजन पर भानू
लील्यो ताहि मधुर फ़ल जानू॥१८॥

Yug sahasra yojan par bhanu
Lilyo taahi madhur phal jaanu

प्रभु मुद्रिका मेलि मुख माही
जलधि लाँघि गए अचरज नाही॥१९॥

Prabhu mudrikaa meli mukh mahi
Jaladhi landhi gaye achraj nahin

दुर्गम काज जगत के जेते
सुगम अनुग्रह तुम्हरे तेते॥२०॥

Durgam kaj jagat ke jete
Sugam anugraha tumhare tete

राम दुआरे तुम रखवारे
होत न आज्ञा बिन पैसारे॥२१॥

Ram duare tum rakhvare
hoatnaagya bina paisare

सब सुख लहैं तुम्हारी सरना
तुम रक्षक काहू को डरना॥२२॥

Sab sukh lahai tumhari sarna
tum rakshak kahu ko darna

आपन तेज सम्हारो आपै
तीनों लोक हाँक तें काँपै॥२३॥

Aapan tej samharo apai
Tinon lokh ankate kanpai

भूत पिशाच निकट नहि आवै
महावीर जब नाम सुनावै॥२४॥

Bhoot pishaach nikat nahin avai
Mahabir jab naam sunavain

नासै रोग हरे सब पीरा
जपत निरंतर हनुमत बीरा॥२५॥

Nasain rog harai sab pira
Japat nirantar hanumat bira

संकट ते हनुमान छुडावै
मन क्रम वचन ध्यान जो लावै॥२६॥

Sankat se hanuman chhudaavei
Man kram vachan dhyan jo laaven

सब पर राम तपस्वी राजा
तिन के काज सकल तुम साजा॥२७॥

Sab par raam tapasvi raja
Tinke kaj sakal tum saja

और मनोरथ जो कोई लावै
सोई अमित जीवन फल पावै॥२८॥

Aur manorath jo koi lavai
Soyi amit jivan phal pavai

चारों युग प्रताप तुम्हारा
है प्रसिद्ध जगत उजियारा॥२९॥

Charo yug Pratap tumhara
Hai prasidh jagat ujiyara

साधु संत के तुम रखवारे
असुर निकंदन राम दुलारे॥३०॥

Sadhu santke tum rakhvare
asurnikandan ram dulare

अष्ट सिद्धि नौ निधि केदाता
अस वर दीन जानकी माता॥३१॥

Asht siddhi navanidhike data
Asabardeenah jaanki maata

राम रसायन तुम्हरे पासा
सदा रहो रघुपति के दासा॥३२॥

Raamrasaayan tumhare pasa
Sada raho Raghupati ke dasa

तुम्हरे भजन रामको पावै
जनम जनम के दुख बिसरावै॥३३॥

Tumhare bhajan ram ko paavai
Janam janam ke dukh bisaravai

अंत काल रघुवर पुर जाई
जहाँ जन्म हरिभक्त कहाई॥३४॥

Antakal raghuvar pur jai
Jahan janma hari bhakta kahai

और देवता चित्त ना धरई
हनुमत सेई सर्व सुख करई॥३५॥

Aurdevta chit nadharai
hanumat sei sarva sukh karai

संकट कटै मिटै सब पीरा
जो सुमिरै हनुमत बलबीरा॥३६॥

Sankata katai mite sab pira
Jo sumrai hanumat balbira

जय जय जय हनुमान गोसाईं
कृपा करहु गुरु देवकी नाई॥३७॥

Jai Jai Jai hanuman gusain
Kripa karahu guru Devaki nain

ये शत बार पाठ कर जोई
छूटहि बंदि महासुख होई॥३८॥

Yah shat bar path karjoi
Chhootahin bandi maha sukh hoi

जो यह पढ़े हनुमान चालीसा
होय सिद्ध साखी गौरीसा॥३९॥

Jo yah padhai hanuman chalisa
hoi siddhi saakhi gaurisa

तुलसीदास सदा हरि चेरा
कीजै नाथ हृदय मह डेरा॥४०॥

Tulsidas sadaa harichera
Kijai nath hridai maha dera

दोहा
Doha

पवन तनय संकट हरन
मंगल मूरति रूप।
राम लखन सीता सहित
हृदय बसहु सुर भूप॥

**Pavan tanai sankat haran
mangalmurati roop
Ram lakhan sita sahit
hridai basahu sur bhoop**

2. Summarised version of the Sundara Kandam

These verses have been extracted from the Valmiki Ramayan. The Sundara Kandam – means the chapter dedicated to Sundara - Hanuman's first name. A lesser known fact is that Hanuman was not his real name – in Sanskrit, it means a person with a broken jaw which Sundara had after a fight with Lord Indra.

The Sundara Kandam describes Hanuman flying to Lanka, meeting Seeta, giving her Rama's ring, meeting Ravana, etc. and ends with him flying back to India, confirming to Rama that Seeta has been kidnapped to Lanka and giving Seeta's hair jewel – the Choodamani as proof that he has indeed met Seeta.

This entire episode happens in 24 hours – from sunset to sunset. Therefore, it is believed that reciting the Sundara Kandam will grant our wishes very quickly. However, it is too long a chapter to be completed in 24 hours.

Below is a summarized version of the Sundara Kandam. It contains 9 verses, which are the essence of the entire chapter and will give the same results as reading the whole Sundara Kandam.

ततोरावणनीतायाःसीतायाःशत्रुकर्शनः इयेषपदमन्वेष्टुंचारणाचरितेपथि

Tato raavana neetaayaah seetaayaah shatru karshanah
Iyesha pada manveshttum chaarana charate pathi

यस्यत्वेतानिचत्वारिवानरेन्द्रयथातव स्मृतिर्मतिर्द्वुतिर्दक्ष्यंस कर्मसु न सीदति

Yasya   tvetaani   chatvaari   vanarendra yathaatava
Smrutir matir drutir daakshyam sakarmasuna seedati

अनिर्वेदहश्रियोमूलंअनिर्वेदहपरंसुखं
अनिर्वेदोहिसततंसर्वार्थेषुप्रवर्तकह

Anirvedhah shriyormoolam anirvedah param
sukham
Anirvedo hi satatam sarvaarteshu
pravartakahaa

नमोस्तुरामायसलक्ष्मणाय देव्यै च
तस्यैजनकात्मजायै
नमोस्तुरुद्रेन्द्रयमानिलेभ्यह
नमोस्तुचंद्रार्कमरुद्गणेभ्यह

Namostu raamaaya salakshmanaaya
Devyaicha tasyai janakaatmajaayai
Namostu rudrendra yamaanilebhyah
Namostu chandraarka marutganebhyah

प्रियन्नसंभवेद्दुखम्अप्रियादधिकंभयं
ताभ्याम्हि ए वियुज्यंतेनमस्त्येषाम्महात्मनाम्

Priyaanna samshavet duhkham apriyaad
adhikambhayam
Taabhyaam hi ye viyujyante namasteshaam
mahaatmanaam

रामःकमलपत्राक्षसर्वसत्वमनोहरः
रूपदाक्षिण्यसंपन्नप्रसूतोजनकात्मजे

Raamah kamalapatraaksha sarvasatva manohara
Roopadaakshinya sampanna prasooto janakaatmaje

जयत्यतिबलोरामलक्ष्मणाश्चमहाबलः
दासोहंकोसलेंद्रस्यरामस्याक्लिष्टकर्मणः

Jayatyatibalo raama lakshmanaascha mahabalaha
Daasoham kosalendrasya raamasyaaklishta karmana

यद्यस्तिपतिशुश्रूषायद्यस्तिचरितंतपः
यदिवास्त्येकपत्नीत्वम्सीतोभवहनूमतह

Yadyasti pati shushrushaa yadyasti charitam tapah
Yadi vaasti ekapatneetvam seetho bhava hanoomatah

निवृत्तवनवासंतंत्वयासार्धमरिंदमं
अभिषिक्तमयोध्यायंक्षिप्रम्द्रक्ष्यसिराघवं

Nivruttavanavaasam tam tvayaa Saardha arindamam
Abhishiktamayodhyaayaam kshipram drakshyasi raghavam

3. Yantrodharaka Hanuman Stotram

Lord Vishnu guarantees that one's wishes will be fulfilled in 6 months

There is a temple in the city of Hampi on the top of a small hill. This is the Yantrodharaka Hanuman temple. The main shrine in the temple is a Yantra with a figure of Hanuman in the middle of it. A Yantra is a geometrical symbol through which any aspect of the Supreme can be bound to any spot for the purpose of worship. This Yantra was created by the great saint Sri Vyasaraya and binds Hanuman in it.

The story goes that once when the great saint was meditating, he felt the presence of Hanuman there. He immediately drew an image of Hanuman on a rock. At once, a monkey leapt out of the image and ran away, and the image vanished. He drew the image of Hanuman again, and once again, a monkey leapt out of it and ran away while also erasing the drawing. Sri Vyasarayaru repeated this 12 times, and each time, a monkey would appear out of the image and erase it.

Finally, he drew a yantra around the image of Hanuman, binding him and ensuring that Hanuman remained there forever. A temple has now come up around the rock on which Sri

Vyasarayaru drew the yantra with Hanuman in the middle of it.

Vyasarayaru also wrote the famous Yantrodharaka Hanuman stotram here. It is said that chanting this mantra 3 times a day will ensure that all one's wishes are fulfilled in 6 months. It is also said that Lord Vishnu himself guarantees that this will work!

नमामिद्दूतंरामस्यसुखदं च सुरद्रुमम्
पीनवृत्तमहाबाहुं सर्वशतृनिवारणं

Namami dootham ramasya sukhadam cha suradrumam
Peenevritha mahabaahum sarva shathru nivaranam

नानारत्नसमायुक्तंकुंडलादिविराजितम्
सर्वदाभीष्ठदातरांसतांवैधृढमावहे

Naanaaratna samaayukta kundalaadhi viraajitam
sarvadaabheesta dhataram sathamvydrida mahave

वासिनंचक्रतीर्थस्यदक्षिणस्थगिरौसदा
तुंगांबोधितरंगस्यवातेनपरिशोभिते

Vaasinam chakratheerthasya dakshinastham girousadha

thungaambhodi tharangasya vaathena
parishobhithe

नानादेशगतैःसद्भिःसेव्यमानंनृपोत्तमैः
धूपदीपादिनैवेद्यैपंचखाद्यैश्चशक्तितः

Naana desha gatheih sadbhihisevyamaanam
nripothamaihi
dhoopa deepadhi neivedyai
panchakaadhyascha shakthithah

भजामिश्रीहनूमतंहेमकांतिसमप्रभम्
व्यासतीर्थयतींद्रेणपूजितंप्रणिधानतः

Bhajaami sri hanumantham hemakaanthi
samaprabham
vyasatheertha yatheendranam poojitham
pranidhaanathaha

त्रिवारंयःपठेत्रित्यंस्तोत्रंभक्त्याद्विजोत्तमः
वांछितंलभतेभीष्टंषण्मासाभ्यंतरेखलु

Thrivaaram yah patennithyam sthothram
bhakthya dwijothama
vanchitham labathe bhistam shanmasa
byantharekalu

पुत्रार्थिलभतेपुत्रान्यशार्थिलभतेयशः
विद्यार्थिलभतेविद्यांधनार्थिलभतेधनं

Putrarthi labhathe putra yashorthi labhathe
yashaha
vidhyaarthi labhathe vidhyam dhanaarthi
labhathe dhanam

सर्वथामास्तुसंदेहोहरिःसाक्षीजगत्पतिः
यःकरोत्यत्रसंदेहंसयातिनरकंधृवम्

Sarvatha Maasthu Sandeho Harihi Sakshi
Jagathpathihi
Yah Karothyathra Sandeham Sayathi
Narakam Dhruvam

AMAZINGLY POWERFUL MANTRAS

7. PRAYERS TO LORD SUBRAMANYA

1. Shanmugha Kavacham – For protection of all kinds

Shanmuga kavacham (Kavacham means a shield) is a powerful hymn composed by Shri. Paamban Swami in 1891 for the benefit of Lord Shanmugha's (who is also known as Subramanya or Murugan) devotees to protect them from illness of body and mind as well as from foes, wild beasts, poisonous creatures, demons, devils and biting insects. There are several instances proving the effectiveness of this mantra. If you recite it with heart and soul to Lord Murugan, the results will be swift and miraculous.

नारदादि देव योगि बृंदाहृद्रिकेतनं
बर्हि वार्य वाहमिंदु शेखरेष्ट नंदनं
भक्त शोक रोग दुःख पाप संग भंजनम्
भावयामि सिंधुतीर वासिनं षडाननं

Naradadhi deva yogi brunda hrud
nikethanam
Barhi varya vahamindu shekareshta
nandanam
Bhaktha shoka roga dukha paapa sanga
banjanam
Bhavayami sindhutheera vasinam
shadananam

तारकारि मिंद्र मुख्य देवबृंदवंदितं
चंद्र चंदनादि शीतलांग मत्मभावितम्
यक्षसिद्ध किन्नरादि मुख्यदिव्य पूजितं
भावयामि सिंधुतीर वासिनं षडाननं

Tharakari mindra mukhya deva brunda
vanditham
Chandra chandanadhi sheethalanga
mathmabhavitham
Yakshasidha kinnaradhi mukhyadivya
poojitham
Bhavayami sindhutheera vasinam
shadananam

चंपकाज्य मालती सुमत्विमल्य भूषितं
दिव्य षड्किरीट हार कुंडलद्य लंकृतं
कुंकुमादि युक्तदिव्य गंध भंग लेपितं
भावयामि सिंधुतीर वासिनं षडाननं

Champakabhja malathee sumatdhimalya
bhooshitham
Divya shad kireeda hara kundaldhya
langrutham
Kumkumadhi yukthadivya ganda bhanga
lepitham
Bhavayami sindhutheera vasinam
shadananam

आश्रिताखिलेष्ट लोकरक्षण मरंग्रुपम्
शक्तिफणीम् अच्युतेंद्र पद्मसंभवादिपं
शिष्टलोक चिंतित सिद्धि दाना लोलुपं
भावयामि सिंधुतीर वासिनं षडाननं

Asrithakhileshta lokarakshana marangripam
Shakthipanim achyuthendra
padmasambhavadhipam
Sishtaloka chinthitha sidhi daana lolupam
Bhavayami sindhutheera vasinam
shadananam

वीरबाहु पूर्वकोटि वीरसंघ सौख्यदाम्
सूरपद्म मुख्य लक्ष कोटिसूर मुक्तिधाम्
इंद्र पूर्व देवसंघ सिद्धनित्य सौख्यधाम्
भावयामि सिंधुतीर वासिनं षडाननं

Veerabahu poorvakoti veerasangha
soukyadham
Soorapadma mukhya laksha kotisoora
mukthidham
Indra poorva devasangha sidhanithya
soukhyadham
Bhavayami sindhutheera vasinam
shadananam

जंब वैरो कामिनी मनोरद पिपूर्वकं
कुंभ संभवायसर्व धर्म सरदायकम्
तंभवाब्धि भोदमंभि गेयमसुसिद्धितं
भावयामि सिंधुतीर वासिनं षडाननं

Jamba vairo kaminee manoradha
pipoorvakam
Kumbha sambhavayasarva dharma
saradaayakam
Thambhavabdhi bodamambhi
geyamasusiddhitham
Bhavayami sindhutheera vasinam
shadananam

पूर्णचंद्र बिंबकोटितुल्य वक्त्रपंकजं
वर्णनीय सच्चरित्रमीश सिद्धिदायकम्
स्वर्ण वर्ण गात्र मुग्र सिद्धलोक शीक्षकं
भावयामि सिंधुतीर वासिनं षडाननं

Poornachandra bimbakotithulya
vakthrapankajam
Varnaneeya sacharithrameesha
sidhidhayakam
Swarna varna gathra mugra sidhaloka
sikshakam
Bhavayami sindhutheera vasinam
shadananam

पूर्वजन्म संचिताग संघभंग तत्परं
सर्व धर्म दान कर्म पूर्व पुण्य सिद्धितं
सर्व शत्रु संघ भंग दक्षमिंद्र चापतिम्
भावयामि सिंधुतीर वासिनं षडाननं

Poorvajanma sanchithaga sangabhanga
thathparam
Sarva dharma daana karma poorva punya
sidhitham
Sarva shathru sanga bhanga dakshamindra
jaapatheem
Bhavayami sindhutheera vasinam
shadananam

2. Shanmugha Maha Mantram - To overcome ill affects of rahu mahadasha in the horoscope

This mantra is especially useful for people who have Rahu in a weak spot in their horoscope or are going through the Rahu mahadasha or Rahu sub-dasha in their horoscope. Reciting it daily will please the Serpent God Rahu. It will definitely reduce the ill effects of this period and help us to find a path/solution and give us the confidence to face the situation.

गणपतिशारदागुरुभ्योनमः
Ganapati sharada gurubhyo namaha

द्विषदभुजं शनमुखम्
अम्बिकासुतम्कुमारम
आदित्य समान तेजसम्
वन्दे मयूरासनं
अग्नि सम्भवम्
सेनान्यम् आद्यम्
ममछाइष्ठी सिद्ध येत

Dwishadbhujam shanmukham
Ambikaasutham kumaaram
Aditya samaana thejasam
Vande mayuraasanam
Agni sambhavam senaanyam aadhyam
Mamachaishti siddha yeth

8. PRAYERS TO THE SUN GOD OR LORD SURYA

1. To get spiritually uplifted and improvement in all walks of life

Gayatri is a wondrous light. Gayatri is one of three feminine names of the Sun God, i.e. Gayatri, Savitri, and Saraswati.

The Gayatri mantra is the mother of all mantras. It describes the supreme reality in the form of light. It does not mention anyone deity or God. It is common to all religions. It addresses the one single absolute energy or God or the supreme power that creates, sustains and dissolves the universe. So, the Gayatri mantra is also called the universal mantra. It is a highly scientific mantra, as confirmed by several studies and research conducted on its chanting.

This mantra is the personification of the Vedas and could also be termed as the summary of all the Vedas. It can be recited at any time of the day. Chanting the Gayatri mantra gives the complete benefit of chanting all the Vedas. A well-known verse about Gayatri mantra says, "Gayan Trayate Iti Gayatri," meaning Gayatri mantra is the one that protects those who chant it.

Gayatri mantra chanting makes the brain sharper and clears confusions in the mind. It gives the devotees the power of making the right decisions and the right judgment and removes all fears and diseases and enhances happiness, wealth and prosperity. It also increases the capacity to focus and learn, making students shine in their studies and elders to shine in their careers.

The pressure on tongue, lips, vocal cord, palate, and the connecting regions in the brain generated by the chanting of the Gayatri mantra creates a vibration that stimulates the hypothalamus - a gland that is responsible for many of our bodily functions including one's power of immunity. This gland is also responsible for the release of happy hormones and is one of the links between the mind and body. A happy person is a healthy person!

The Gayatri mantra also acts as a cardiac and nerve tonic as the vibrations stimulate vital points on the heart and nerves. As it increases blood circulation and gets rid of toxins, it oxygenates the skin, making it look younger and glowing.

Gayatri Maha Mantra

ॐ भूर्भुवः स्वाहा
तत्सवितुर्वरेण्यम्
भर्गो देवस्य धीमहि
धियोयोनः प्रच्छोदयात

Om bhurbhuvah swaha
Thath savithur varenyam
Bhargo devasya dheemahi
Dheeyoyonah prachodayaath

2. **To face and overcome enemies and self-destructive behaviour**

Worshipping the Sun God is well known in many civilisations and has been around since time immemorial. The Sun is a God that we can physically see. His rays sustain us. The Aditya Hridayam is a Mantra dedicated to the Sun God or Surya. The benefits of reciting the Aditya

Hridayam are several.

In the last chapter of the Ramayana, Rama fights with Ravana for 9 days and is unable to defeat him. After the 9th day of war, he sits dejected that he is unable to fulfil his life's purpose. Just then, the great Sage Agastya arrives and advises Rama to chant the Aditya Hridayam stothra at sunrise and then go to battle with Ravana. The next morning Rama recites the Aditya Hridayam with devotion and then goes to the war front and, as is well known – he succeeds in vanquishing Ravana.

This mantra is to be recited only before 12 Noon. It is said that the benefits are reversed if recited after 12 Noon.

People who recite the Aditya Hridayam get a divine Aura around them. This Mantra gives us the confidence to face our internal and external enemies and conquer them. It is a powerful tool that we can carry with us all the time to fight off our enemies.

According to the Srimad Bhagavatam, Satrajit obtained the Shyamantaka gem by worshipping Surya and got unimaginable wealth. Yudhistira obtained an Akshaya Patra by worshipping Lord Surya. This was a wishfulfilling bowl and gave its owner unlimited food and necessities.

It is also well known that the Sun is a powerful and quick healer. An open wound if left to face the Sun heals quickly without becoming septic or further infected. Reciting this powerful mantra is said to cure many ailments, including skin problems and leprosy.

The Skanda Purana mentions that one has to pray to God Surya for happiness and welfare.

Aditya Hridayam Prayer

जटायु जटायु सूर्यम्
सप्तलोकैक दीपम्
किरणशमिता पापक्लेश
दुःखस्य नाशम्

Jatayu jatayu sooryam
Saptalokaika deepam
Kiranashmita paapaklesha
Dukhasya naasham

अरुणकिरण गम्यम
आदिम आदित्यमूर्तिम
सकला भुवनवंद्यम्
भास्कम् तम् नमामि

Arunakirana gamyam
Aadim aadityamoortim
Sakala bhuvanavandhyam
Bhaskaram tam namaami

Aditya Hridayam

ततो युद्धपरिश्रान्तं समरे चिन्तया स्थितम्।
रावणं चाग्रतो दृष्ट्वा युद्धाय समुपस्थितम्॥१॥

Tato yuddhaparishraantam
Samare chintayaa sthitam
Raavanam jaagrato drshtvaa
Yuddhaaya samupasthitam

देवतैश्च समागम्य द्रष्टुमभ्यागतोरणम्।
उपागम्याब्रवीद्रामम गस्त्यो भगवानृषिः॥२॥

Devataishcha samaagamya
Drashtumabhyaagatoranam
Upagamyaabraveedraamam
Agastyo bhagavaan rshihi

अगस्तयोवाचा
AgastyoVaacha

राम राम महा बाहो शृणु गुह्यं सनातनम्।
येन सर्वानरीन्वत्स समरे विजयिष्यसि॥३॥

Raama Raama maha baaho
Shrunu guhyam sanaatanam
Ena sarvaanareen vatsa
Samare vijayishyasi

आदित्य हृदयं पुण्यंसर्वशत्रु विनाशनम्।
जयावहं जपेन्नित्यमक्षय्यं परमंशिवम्॥४॥

Aditya hridayam punyam
Sarvashatru vinaashanam
Jayaavaham japennityam
Akshayam paramam shivam

सर्व मङ्गल माङ्गल्यं सर्व पाप प्रणाशनम्।
चिन्ता शोक प्रशमनमायुर्वर्धनमुत्तमम्॥५॥

Sarva mangala maangalyam
Sarva paapa pranaashanam
Chinta shoka prashamanam
Aayurvadhanam Uttamam

रश्मिमन्तंसमुद्यन्तं देवासुर नमस्कृतम्।
पूजयस्व विवस्वन्तं भास्करं भुवनेश्वरम्॥६॥

Rashmimantam samudyantam
Devaasura namakrutam
Poojayasva vivasvantam
Bhaskaram bhuvaneshwaram

सर्वदेवात्मको ह्येषः तेजस्वी रश्मि भावनः।
एष देवासुरगणान्लोकान्पाति गभस्तिभिः॥७॥

Sarvadevaatmako hyeshaha
Tejasvee rashmi bhaavanaha
Esha devaasuraganaan
Lokaan paati gabhastibhihi

एष ब्रह्मा च विष्णुश्चशिवः स्कन्दः प्रजापतिः।
माहेन्द्रो धनदः कालो यमस्सोमोह्यपांपतिः॥८॥

Esha brahmaash cha vishnush cha
Shiva skandah prajaapatihi
Mahendro dhanadah kaalo
Yamah somo hyapaam patihi

पितरो वसवस्साध्याःह्यश्विनौमरुतोमनुः ।
वायुर्वह्निः प्रजाप्राणा ऋतुकर्ता प्रभाकरः ॥९॥

Pitaro vasavaha saadhyaa
Hyashivinou maruto manuhu
Vaayurvahnih prajaapraanaha
Rutukartaa prabhaakaraha

आदित्यः सविता सूर्यः खगः पूषा गभस्तिमान् ।
सुवर्ण सदृशोभानुर्हिरण्यरेतादिवाकरः ॥१०॥

Aaditya svitaa sooryaha
Khagah poosha gabhastimaan
Suvarna sadhyasho bhanur hiranya retaa
divaakaraha

हरिदश्च स्सहस्रार्चि स्सप्तसप्तिर्मरीचिमान् ।
तिमिरोन्मथन शशम्भु स्त्वष्टा मार्ताण्ड
अंशुमान् ॥११॥

Haridashvaha Sahasraarchihi
Saptasaptihi mareechimaan
Timironmathanah shambhu tvashta
Maartanda amshumaan

हिरण्य गर्भशिशिशिरस्तपनो भास्करो रविः।
अग्निगर्भोऽदितेः पुत्रः शङ्ख
शिशिशिरनाशनः ॥१२॥

Hiranya gabhaha shishirastapano
Bhaskaro ravihi
Agnigarbho (a)diteh putraha
Shankha Shishiranaashanaha

व्योमनाथस्तमोभेदीऋग्यजुस्सामपारगः।
घनवृष्टिरपांमित्रोविन्ध्यवीथीप्लवङ्गमः ॥१३॥

Vyomanaathastomobedi
Rig yajur saamapaaragaha
Ghanavrishtirapaam mitro
Vindhyaveethe plavangamaha

आतपी मण्डली मृत्युः पिङ्गलस्सर्वतापनः।
कविर्विश्वो महातेजाः रक्त स्सर्वभवोद्भवः ॥१४॥

Aatapee mandalee mrtyuhu
Pingalaha sarvataapanaha
Kavirvishvo mahaatejaa
Raktah sarvabhavodbhavaha

नक्षत्र ग्रहताराणामधिपोविश्वभावनः।
तेजसामपितेजस्वीद्वादशात्मन्नमोऽस्तुते॥१५॥

Nakshatra grahataaraam adhipo
Vishvabhaavanaha
Tejasaam api tejasvee
Dvaadashaatman namostu te

नमःपूर्वायगिरयेपश्चिमायाद्रयेनमः।
ज्योतिर्गणानांपतयेदिनाधिपतयेनमः॥१६॥

Namah poorvaaya giraye
Paschimaayaadraye namaha
Jyotirgana naam pataye
Dinaadhipataye namaha

जयायजयभद्रायहर्यश्वायनमोनमः।
नमोनमस्सहस्रांशोआदित्यायनमोनमः॥१७॥

Jayaaya jayabhadraaya
Haryashvaaya namo namah
Namo namah sahasraamsho
Aadityaa ya namo namaha

नमउग्रायवीरायसारङ्गायनमोनमः।
नमःपद्मप्रमोधायमार्तण्डायनमोनमः॥१८॥

Namah ugraaya veeraaya
Saarangaaya namo namaha
Namaha padmapramodhaaya

Maartaandaaya namo namah

ब्रह्मेशानाच्युतेशायसूर्यादित्यवर्चसे।
भास्वतेसर्वभक्षायरौद्रायवपुषेनमः॥१९॥

Brahmeshaanaachyuteshaaya
Sooryaadityavarcha se
Bhaasvate sarvabhakshaaya
Rowdraaya vapushe namaha

तमोघ्नायहिमघ्नायशत्रुघ्नायामितात्मने।
कृतघ्नघ्नायदेवायज्योतिषांपतयेनमः॥२०॥

Tamoghnaaya himaghnaaya
Shatrughnaaya amitaatmane
Krutaghnaghnaaya devaaya
Jyotishaam pataye namaha

तप्तचामीकराभायवह्नयेविश्वकर्मणे।
नमस्तमोऽभिनिघ्नायरवियेलोकसाक्षिणे॥२१॥

Taptachaameekaraabhaaya
Vahnaye vishvakarmane
Namastom (a)bhighnaaya
Raviye lokassakshine

नाशयत्येषवैभूतंतदेवसृजतिप्रभुः।
पायत्येषतपत्येषवर्षत्येषगभस्तिभिः॥२२॥

Naashayatyesha vai bhootam
Tadev srijati prabhuhu
Paayatyesha tapatyesha
Varshatyesha gabhastibhihi

एषसुप्तेषुजागर्तिभूतेषुपरिनिष्ठितः।
एषएवाग्निहोत्रंचफलंचैवाग्निहोत्रिणाम्॥२३॥

Esha supteshu jaagarti
Bhooteshu parinishthitaha
Esha evaagnihotram cha
Phalam chaivaagnihotrinaam

वेदाश्चक्रतवश्चैवक्रतूनांफलमेवच।
यानिकृत्यानिलोकेषुसर्वएषरविःप्रभुः॥२४॥

Vedaascha kratavashchaiva
Kratoonaam phalameva cha
Yaani krtyaani lokeshu
Sarva esha ravihi prabhuhu

एनमापत्सुकृच्छ्रेषुकान्तारेषुभयेषुच।
कीर्तयन्पुरुषःकश्चिन्नावसीदतिराघव॥२५॥

Enamaapatsu krchepshu
Kaantaareshu bhayeshu cha
Keertayan purushaha

Kashchhinaavaseedati raghava

पूजयस्वैनमेकाग्रोदेवदेवंजगत्पतिम्।
एतत्त्रिगुणितंजप्त्वायुद्धेषुविजयिष्यसि॥२६॥

Poojayasvaina mekaagro
Devadevam jagath patim
Etat trigunitam japtaa
Yuddheshu vijayishyasi

अस्मिन्क्षणेमहाबाहोरावणंत्वंवधिष्यसि।
एवमुक्त्वाततोऽगस्त्योजगमाच यथागतम्॥२७॥

Asminkshshane mahaabaaho
Raavanam tvam vadhishyasi
Evamkuktvaa tadaagastyo
Jagamaa cha yathaagatham

एतच्छुत्वामहातेजाःनष्टशोकोऽभवत्तदा।
धारयामाससुप्रीतोराघवः प्रयतात्मवान्॥२८॥

Etachchurtvaa mahaatejaa
Nashtashoko (a)bhavaattadha
Dhaaryaamaasa supreeto
Raghavaha prayataatmavaan

आदित्यंप्रेक्ष्यजप्त्वातुपरंहर्षमवाप्तवान्।
त्रिराचम्यशुचिभूर्त्वाधनुरादायवीर्यवान्॥२९॥

Aadityam preksha japtvaa tu
Param harshamavaaptvaan
Triraachamya shuchirbhotvaa
Dhanuradaaya veeryavaan

रावणंप्रेक्ष्यहृष्टात्मायुद्धायसमुपागमत्।
सर्वयत्नेनमहतावधेतस्यधृतोऽभवत्॥३०॥

Raavanam prekshya hrushtattmaa
Yuddhaaya samupaagamat
Sarvayatnena mahataa vadhe
Tasya dhrto(a)bhagavat

अथरविरवदत्निरीक्ष्यराममंमुदितमनाःपरमंप्रहृष्यमा
णः।
निशिचरपतिसंक्षयंविदित्वासुरगणमध्यगतोवच
स्त्वरेति॥३१॥

Atha ravira vadana nireekshya raamam
Mudita maanaha paramam
prahrushyamaanaha
Nishi charapati samkshayam viditvaa
Suragana madhyagato vachastraveti

इतिश्रीमदरामायणेवाल्मीकिआदिकव्येयुधाकांडे
आदित्यहृदयस्तोत्रम्सम्पूर्णम्

Iti Srimad Ramayane Valmiki Adikavye
Yuddakaande Aditya Hridaya Stotram
Sampoornam

9. OTHER MANTRAS

1. Powerful Mantra for Meditation

The mantra OM is made of three syllables = Aa, Oo, and Mm. It is the first word ever created. It is said that the outer space reverberates with the sound of OM. It is a universal mantra and purifies the environment with its positive vibrations.

Chanting of the Om mantra increases one's concentration, immunity, and self healing power. The chanting of this sound creates vibrations through the lips, tongue, palate, back of the throat, and skull, which helps in the release of relaxing hormones and calming the mind. It produces vibration and sound, which is also felt through our vocal cords and sinuses. The vibrations open up the sinuses to clear the airways and strengthen the vocal cords. Meditating on OM produces deep relaxation because of which our blood pressure decreases, and our heart beats with a regular rhythm. If we rub our hands together while chanting OM and put those charged hands on different parts of the body we can heal or activate those areas of the body. If we concentrate on the third or spiritual eye while chanting, our eyesight will improve. Our power of intuition also improves exponentially.

The sound Aaaa is generated from the abdomen. It helps to strengthen the supporting muscles of the spinal cords, which in turn strengthen the spinal cord itself.

The sound Oooo is created by the vocal cords, and this greatly benefits the thyroid glands and the throat.

The sound Mmmm is the sound of infinity and ends in a deep silence which energises and uplifts our emotions. We will have better control over our emotions, thus allowing us to see situations with a clear and rational mind.

Studies have shown that the increase in levels of internal positive energy and a cleansed aura that come from chanting the Om mantra regularly will be reflected with a sunny glow on our face and body.

ॐ   ॐ   ॐ   ॐ   ॐ   ॐ

OM...... OM..... OM...... OM...... OM...... OM......

2. Prayers to Kanchi Periya Mahaswami

Kanchi Periya Mahaswami was the 68th Head of the Kanchi Kamokoti Math in Kancheepuram. He is also known as Periyava, the Sage of Kanchi, Mahaswami, etc. and is considered as an incarnation of Shiva himself. He has given us valuable discourses on various aspects of life, and the people of South India consider his words as "Veda Vaaku," which means equivalent to the Vedas.

A few years before he attained Siddhi, the priests of the Nataraja temple in Chidambaram came to meet Periyavaa and brought with them the Kunjitha Paadam garland. The Kunjitha Paadam is a special garland made of several herbs and roots, and it is placed on the main idol of Lord Nataraja in the holy city of Chidambaram. It is a belief that a darshan of this Kunjitha Paadam will cure a person of all diseases and that it will enable him/her to attain Moksha or salvation.

As soon as it was brought in, Periyava took the Kunjitha Paadam and kept it on His head, and blessed all the onlookers. The photo that was taken at that moment is believed to be a great cure for any disease, as it contains the medicine (Kunjitha Paadam) and the greatest of all doctors (Sri Maha Periyava) together in one photo. This photo is available on the internet. The below mantra is about Maha Periyavaa and the Kunjitha Paadam garland.

This mantra can heal any physical problem. It works on the kidneys when it does not function very well. When there is breathlessness, please recite this mantra. It works on the heart muscles – as if searching for the inner heart. If you would like to find the inner soul also, you can chant this mantra. It can be chanted for any acute or chronic, physical, or mental disorder. The Kunjitha Paadam mantra has the capability to control hysteric people and in the management of schizophrenic patients.

In cases where doctors are unable to diagnose the illness or where there are unforeseen complications, this mantra will help. It will even work remotely if someone we care about is unwell or has been hospitalised! This is a small yet very powerful mantra.

कुंचित शंकर ध्यानम्
सर्व रोग निवारनिम्
कुंचित शंकर पाद शरणम्

Kunchitha shankara dhyaanam
Sarva roga nivaaraneem
Kunchitha shankara pada sharanam

3. To live a long and bountiful life

The Buddha Amitayus is a celestial Buddha who is most often described in the sacred texts that belong to the Buddhism school known as the Mahayana school. He is one of the manifestations of Amitabha, who is closely associated with longevity. Amitayus is described and illustrated in a seated position, with his hands holding onto a vessel that contains Amrita the nectar of immortality. The leaves of the Ashoka tree also feature prominently, as this tree is said to symbolize a long life that is free from the suffering that disease inflicts on our physical forms.

The name Amitayus can be easily understood when broken down into two parts.

Amita means infinite or everlasting
Ayus means life or existence

Thus Amitayus' name can be translated to mean

"one with boundless life" or "he whose life is infinite." His name can also be understood as infinite light. He is the principal Buddha for overcoming the power that death and ignorance have over us. With these removed, we can fulfil our true human potential which is the achievement of true happiness and Nirvana.

In the sutras that Buddha Sakyamuni wrote, he spoke about the great power and the benefits that the mantra of Buddha Amitayus can offer us. The sutras go on to describe just how intensely powerful the mantra is, with reciting it just once is akin to ninety-nine million Buddhas chanting the mantra themselves.

Buddha Amitayus is the Buddha who gives us boundless merit, life, and wisdom. By reciting the mantra of Amitayus, we will be able to develop our own qualities of wisdom, life, and boundless merit, all of which are required for our spiritual development. This will ultimately help us to achieve true enlightenment. This mantra also eliminates the obstacles that are in our way of achieving a long life. These obstacles could be a pain, sickness, or untimely or premature death. It is said to also be helpful for those who are expecting a baby but who may have suffered from a miscarriage in the past.

Amitayus and all that he represents is an essential part of any journey towards enlightenment because longevity is an essential factor that will permit us all the extra time that we need to work through our elimination of suffering in our quest for enlightenment. The practice of Amitayus can also help us to remove the obstacles that could endanger the lives of those we care for.

Reciting the below mentioned short and simple, very powerful Amitayus mantra should be an essential part of our journey towards seeking enlightenment. The mantra will not only help us with the elimination of some of the suffering from our life, but it will also help us to understand what it means to be truly enlightened.

बुद्ध अमित आयुष
बुद्ध अमित आयुष
बुद्ध अमित आयुष

Buddha Amit Ayush
Buddha Amit Ayush
Buddha Amit Ayush

4. To rid oneself of negative karmas

The benefits of reciting Om Mani Padme Hum are like the infinite sky. Reciting Om Mani Padme Hum even once can purify negative karma. So it is very powerful

Om - purifies the ego
Ma - purifies jealousy
Ni - purifies passion
Pad - purifies ignorance
Me - purifies greed
Hum - purifies hatred

Tibetan Buddhists believe that saying this mantra Om Mani Padme Hum, out loud or silently to oneself, calls upon the powerful benevolent attention and blessings of Chenrezig, who is the embodiment of compassion. The benefits of reciting the Compassion Buddha mantra are incalculable.

If a person who chants this six-syllable mantra of Compassion Buddha just once a day, goes into a river or sea, the water that touches the person's body gets blessed, and this blessed water then purifies all the billions of living beings in the water. The person has the power to save the animals in that water from pain and suffering.

Similarly, when such a person walks on the road

and wind touches the body of the person and when the wind goes on to touch the insects, their negative karma gets purified. When such a person does touch others, their negative karma also gets purified. It is believed that even the person's breath touching the bodies of other living beings purifies their negative karma.

By chanting this mantra, the body becomes so powerful and blessed that this affects the consciousness of up to seven generations.

This mantra might seem simple to recite, but it will prove to be highly beneficial. It helps us to live a guilt free and beautiful life.

ॐ मणि पद्मे हूं
ॐ मणि पद्मे हूं
ॐ मणि पद्मे हूं

Om Mani Padme Hum
Om Mani Padme Hum
Om Mani Padme Hum

5. Morning mantra – to have a great day

"Have a great day" is a common greeting in today's world. But our heritage has given us a mantra that literally allows us to have a wonderful day. This mantra is to be recited each morning as soon as we wake up. It is a prayer for wealth, wisdom, and happiness.

Please be sure to wake up on the right side of your bed. Then rub both your palms together and slowly open your eyes looking at your open palms and then recite this mantra. Once you finish repeating the mantra, rub your palms together again and wipe your eyes and face with the vibrations caused by reciting this mantra. Feel the positive energy it gives you!

Kara Aagre vasate Lakshmi – in the tip of the palm lives Lakshmi – the God of wealth

Kara Madhye Saraswati – in the middle of the palm resides Saraswati – the God of learning and wisdom

Kara Moole Sthithe Gowri – At the end of the palm resides Gowri or Parvati – the God of power

Prabhaathe Kara Darshanam – Looking at the open palm early in the morning

कराग्रे वसते लक्ष्मी: करमध्ये सरस्वती।
करमूले स्थितेगौरी प्रभाते करदर्शनम्।।

Karagre vasate Lakshmi
Kara madhye Saraswati
Kara moolesthithe Gowri
Prabhaathe karadarshanam

6. To sleep well without any nightmares

When we were little, our parents taught us this mantra to prevent us from waking up in the middle of the night with a nightmare. It also helped us to sleep better when we were stressed out during our exams. The meaning of this mantra is that when we are ready to fall asleep, we think of the Gods Rama, Hanuman, Vynatheya, and Vrukodhara. By doing this, we get good sleep without any nightmares or stress related sleep disorders

रामंस्कन्दं हनूमन्तं वैनतेयं वृकोदरम्।
शयनेयः स्मरेत्रित्यं दुस्वपनम् तस्य नश्यति।।

Ramaskandam Hanumantham Vynatheyam Vrukodharam
Shayaneya Smarenithyam Dhuswapnam Thasya Nashyathi

7. To seek God for His forgiveness for one's offenses

During our prayers, we sometimes lose concentration and pronounce the mantras incorrectly, recite with lack of sufficient devotion, or go into an auto pilot mode and recite without absorbing the meaning of the mantras. The below mentioned mantra seeks God's forgiveness for these mistakes and asks Him to provide us with the benefit of the mantras that we recite despite all these faults. Therefore, it is always a good practice to generally end your prayers with this mantra.

श्री अपराधाशोधन
Sri Aparadhashodhana

मन्त्र हीनम् क्रिया हीनम् भक्ति हीनम् जनार्धना
यत्पूजितम् मयादेवा परिपूर्णम्तदृअस्तुमे

Mantra hinam kriya hinam bhakti hinam janaardana
Yatpujitam mayadeva paripurnam tad astu me

यदक्षर पदभ्रष्टम् मात्राहीनंतुयत्भवेत्
तत्सर्व क्षम्यतांदेव नारायण नमोस्तुते
विसर्ग बिन्दुमात्राणि पाद पादाक्ष राणिच
न्यूनानि चातिरिक्तानि क्षमस्व पुरुषोत्तम

Yadakshara padabrastam maatra heenam tu
yad bhavet
Tat sarvam kshyamyataam deva naraayana
namostute

Visarga bindu maatraani paada paadaa
ksharaani cha
Nyoonaani chatiriktaani kshamasva
purushottama

All the mantras given in this book have the
power to change our lives in ways that we desire.
We can also use some of the mantras for benefits
other than those mentioned in the index. The
description of the mantras within the content gives
us many other uses too. Please use as required.
However, we need to remember that repeated
recitation of the mantras is the key to transforming
one's life. Also, miracles happen when our greatest
asset is faith in the Almighty.

I wish you good luck on your new journey and
pray that you reach your goals very soon.

For help with pronunciation of Mantras please
visit our YouTube Channel -
https://www.youtube.com/channel/UCkTiY1FbUJwfglN
IxCIxdNw

ABOUT THE AUTHOR

Sharada lives in Bengaluru, India. She has been employed in the FMCG and Banking industries for the last three decades. Life has been a roller coaster ride for her. She has had her share of the ups and downs and curve balls that life tends to throw at people.

Sharada firmly believes that her regular prayers, implicit faith in the Almighty and the unconditional love and support of her family helped her to cross the turbulent waters of several critical illnesses (double Pneumonia – to name one of them!), health scares, severe financial distress, and an unpleasant divorce because of which she had to reboot her life and begin afresh with her 10 year old daughter.

She truly believes that "You don't find Mantras; the Mantras find you."

This book is a collection of Mantras that have found her. She is now witnessing her life limping back into normalcy and unfolding into a state of peace and calm that she never thought was possible.

Sharada is an unquestionable proof that these Mantras work.

She lovingly presents all her Mantras to you in the absolute belief that you will benefit from these Mantras as much as it has benefitted her.

Printed in Great Britain
by Amazon